THE BLUEBIRD
CARRIES THE SKY
ON HIS BACK

Henry David Thoreau

THE BLUEBIRD CARRIES THE SKY ON HIS BACK

Henry David Thoreau

Photographs by
Nancy W. Stanford
Eric L. Ergenbright
R. W. Young
Floyd Norgaard

STANYAN BOOKS

RANDOM HOUSE

A Stanyan book
Published by Stanyan Books,
8721 Sunset Blvd., Suite C
Los Angeles, California 90069,
and by Random House, Inc.
201 E. 50th Street,
New York, N.Y. 10022

Designed by Hy Fujita

Printed in U.S.A.

THE BLUEBIRD CARRIES THE SKY ON HIS BACK

Henry David Thoreau

We have lived not in proportion to the number of years we have spent on the earth, but in proportion as we have enjoyed.

The perception of beauty is a moral test.

I went to the woods because I wished to see
if I could not learn what life had to teach —
and not, when I came to die, discover
that I had not lived.

Rather than love, than money, than fame,
give me truth.

The doctrine of despair was never taught by
such as shared the serenity of nature.
The spruce, the hemlock and the pine
will not countenance despair.

That man is the richest whose pleasures
are the cheapest.

Be not simply good; be good for something.

A healthy man is the complement of the seasons,
and in winter, summer is in his heart.

I take an axe and pail and go in search of water . . .
Every winter the liquid and trembling surface of the pond,
which was so sensitive to every breath and reflected
every light and shadow, becomes solid to the depth of a
foot and a half — and perchance the snow covers it to an
equal depth. Like the marmots in the surrounding hills,
it closes its eyelids for three months or more.

I cut my way first through a foot of snow and then a foot of ice, and open a window under my feet where, kneeling to drink, I look down into the quiet parlor of the fishes; there a perennial waveless serenity reigns as in the amber twilight sky, corresponding to the cool and even temperament of the inhabitants. Heaven is under our feet as well as over our heads.

While men believe in the infinite,
some ponds will be thought to be bottomless.

Some circumstantial evidence is very strong,
as when you find a trout in the milk.

The finest qualities in our nature, like the bloom on
fruits, can be preserved only by the most
delicate handling.

Superfluous wealth can buy superfluities only.

Ah, the pickerel of Walden! I am always surprised
by their rare beauty . . . a dazzling and transcendant
beauty. . . . They are not green like the pines,
nor gray like the stones, nor blue like the sky, but
they have yet rare colors, as if they were the pearls,
the animalized *nuclei* or crystals of the Walden
water. . . . It is surprising that they are caught here
—that in this deep spring—far beneath the rattling
trams and chaises and tinkling sleighs that travel
the Walden road, this great gold and emerald
fish swims.

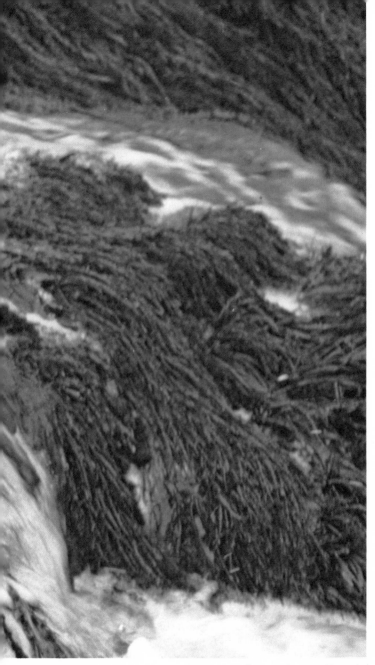

We need the tonic of wildness.

I wonder what the world is doing today.

The rich man is always sold to the institution which makes him rich. Absolutely speaking, the more money the less virtue; for money comes between a man and his objects, and obtains them for him. And it was certainly no great virtue to obtain it.

Money is not required to buy one necessity of the soul.

I please myself with imagining a State at last which can afford to be just to all men, and to treat the individual with respect as a neighbor.

My furniture, part of which I made myself, consisted of a bed, a table, a desk, three chairs, a looking-glass, a pair of tongs and andirons, a kettle, a skillet and frying pan, a dipper, a wash-bowl, two knives and forks, three plates, one cup, one spoon, a jug for oil, a jug for molasses, and a japanned lamp.

Furniture! . . . It is as if all these traps were buckled to a man's belt, and he could not move without dragging them—dragging his trap. . . . Whenever you meet a man you will see all that he owns, ay, and much he pretends to disown, behind him—even to his kitchen furniture and all the trumpery which he saves and will not burn—and he will appear to be harnessed to it.

It costs me nothing for curtains, for I have no gazers to shut out but the sun and moon, and I am willing that they should look in.

Most of the luxuries of life are positive hindrances to the elevation of mankind.

I would rather sit on a pumpkin, and have it all to myself, than to be crowded on a velvet cushion.

The indescribable beneficence of Nature—of sun and wind and rain, of summer and winter—such health, such cheer, they afford forever! Such sympathy have they with our race that all Nature would be affected, and the sun's brightness fade, and the winds would sigh and the clouds rain tears, and the woods shed their leaves and put on mourning in midsummer—if any man should ever for a just cause grieve. Shall I not have intelligence with the earth? Am I not partly leaves and vegetable mould myself?

Morning air! If men will not drink of this at the fountainhead of the day, then we must bottle up some and sell it in the shops, for the benefit of those who have lost their ticket to morning time in this world.

We are wont to forget that the sun looks on our cultivated fields and on the prairies and forests without distinction. They all reflect and absorb his rays alike, and the former make but a small part of the glorious picture which he beholds in his daily course. In his view the earth is all equally cultivated like a garden. Therefore we should receive the benefit of his light and heat with a corresponding trust and magnanimity.

Men learn to read to serve a paltry convenience—
as they learn to cipher in order to keep accounts—
but of reading as a noble intellectual exercise they
know little. They dissipate their faculties in what
is called easy reading.

To a philosopher all *news,* as it is called, is gossip,
and they who edit and read it are old women
over their tea.

For my part, I could easily do without the post
office. I think there are very few important
communications made through it.

I have always regretted I am not as wise as the day I was born.

My greatest skill has been to want but little.

Our life is frittered away by detail.

Why should we live with such hurry and waste of life? We are determined to be starved before we are hungry.

The wind has gently murmured through the blinds, or puffed with feathery softness against the windows—and occasionally sighed like a summer zephyr lifting the leaves along. . . .

While the earth has slumbered, all the air has been alive with feathery flakes as if some northern Ceres reigned, showering her silvery grain over the fields. . . . The snow lies warm as cotton upon the window sill.

The stillness of the morning is impressive. The floor creaks as we move toward the window to look through some clear space over the fields. We see the roofs stand under their snow burden. The trees rear white arms to the sky on every side; and where were walls and fences we see fantastic forms stretching in frolic gambols across the dusky landscape, as if Nature had strewn her fresh designs over the fields by night as models for man's art.

As we stand in the midst of the pines, we wonder if the towns have ever heard their simple story. We borrow from the forest the boards which shelter and the sticks which warm us. . . . What would human life be without forests, those natural cities? From the tops of mountains they appear like smooth-shaven lawns, yet whither shall we walk but in this taller grass?

A pure elastic heaven hangs over all, as if the impurities of the summer sky, refined and shrunk by the chaste winter's cold, had been winnowed from the heavens upon the earth.

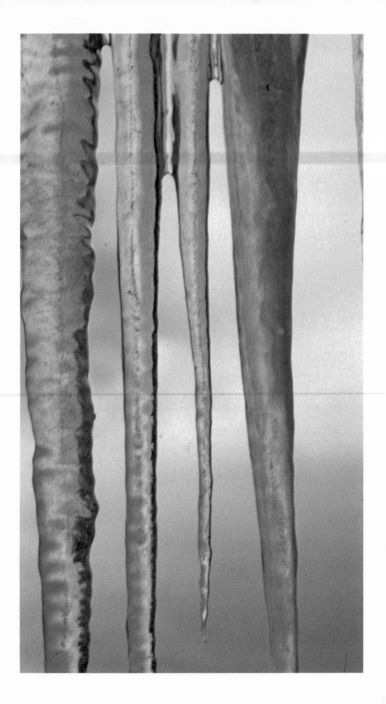

The first ice is especially interesting and perfect,
being hard, dark and transparent, and affords the
best opportunity for examining the bottom where it
is shallow. For you can lie at your length on ice only
an inch thick, and study the bottom at your leisure.
. . . But the ice itself is the object of more interest.
If you examine it closely you find that the bubbles,
which at first appeared to be within it, are against
its under surface, and that more are continually
rising from the bottom. . . . These bubbles are very
clear and beautiful, and you see your face
reflected in them through the ice. . . . Each, in its
degree, operates like a burning-glass on the ice
beneath to melt and rot it. These are the little
air-guns which contribute to make the ice
crack and whoop.

Walden is a perfect forest mirror, set round with stones and precious to my eye.

I rejoice that there are owls. Let them do the idiotic and maniacal hooting for men.

As for conforming outwardly, and living your own life inwardly, I do not think much of that.

There is never an instant's truce between virtue and vice. Goodness is the only investment that never fails.

He is blessed who loses no moment of the passing life in remembering the past.

A man is rich in proportion to the number of things he can afford to let alone.

Even the best things are not equal to their fame.

There are a thousand hacking at the branches of evil to one who is striking at the root.

On Sundays ... when the wind was favorable ... I heard the bells of Concord, a faint, sweet melody, worth importing into the wilderness.

*At a distance over the wood, this sound acquires a
certain vibratory hum, as if the pine needles in the
horizon were the strings of a harp which it swept. . . .
It was partly the voice of the wood.*

*At evening, the distant lowing of some cow in the
horizon beyond the woods sounded sweet and melodious
. . . Regularly, at half past seven in one part of the
summer, the whippoorwills chanted their vespers for
half an hour, sitting on a stump by my door, or upon
the ridgepole of the house.*

*The screech owls' dismal scream . . . is a most solemn
graveyard ditty . . . Wise midnight hags! Yet I love to
hear their wailing trilled along the woodside, as if it
were the dark and tearful side of music, the regrets and
sighs that would fain be sung.*

Water is the only drink for a wise man.

If you have any enterprise before you, try it in your old clothes.

It is life near the bone, where it is sweetest.

By avarice and selfishness and a groveling habit of regarding the soil as property, the landscape is deformed.

Late in the evening all the shore rang with the trump of bullfrogs, the sturdy spirits of ancient wine-bibbers and wassailers, still unrepentant, trying to sing a catch in their Stygian lake.

Night after night the geese came lumbering in in the dark with a clangor and a whistling of wings, even after the ground was covered with snow. Several times . . . I heard the tread of a flock of geese, or else ducks, on the dry leaves in the woods by a pond-hole behind my dwelling where they had come up to feed—and the faint honk or quack of their leader as they hurried off.

We should be blessed if we lived in the present always.
We loiter in winter when it is already spring.

The pond began to boom about an hour after sunrise, when it felt the influence of the sun's rays. It stretched itself and yawned like a waking man with a gradually increasing tumult, which was kept up for three or four hours. It took a short siesta at noon, and boomed once more toward night. . . . In the right stage of the weather a pond fires its evening gun with great regularity. Though I perceive no difference in the weather, the pond does. Who would have suspected so large and cold and thick-skinned a thing to be so sensitive? Yet it has its law to which it thunders obedience.

Ere long, on every hill and plain and in every hollow, the frost comes out of the ground . . . and seeks the sea with music, or migrates to other climes in clouds. Thaw with his gentle persuasion is more powerful than Thor with his hammer.

The infant year just peeping forth with the stately beauty of the withered vegetation which had withstood the winter . . . goldenrods, pinweeds, cottongrass, cat-tails, mulleins, johnswort, hard-tack, meadow-sweet, and other strong-stemmed plants which entertain the earliest birds—decent weeds, at least, which widowed Nature wears.

At the approach of spring the red squirrels got under my house, two at a time, directly under my feet as I sat reading or writing, and kept up the queerest chuckling and chirruping . . . and when I stamped my feet they only chirruped the louder, as if past all fear and respect in their mad pranks, defying humanity to stop them.

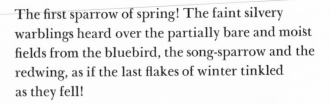

The first sparrow of spring! The faint silvery warblings heard over the partially bare and moist fields from the bluebird, the song-sparrow and the redwing, as if the last flakes of winter tinkled as they fell!

O the evening robin, at the end of a New England summer day!

The grass flames up on the hillsides like a spring fire—as if the earth sent forth an inward heat to greet the returning sun.

The brooks sing carols and glees to the spring.

*A single gentle rain makes the grass
many shades greener.*

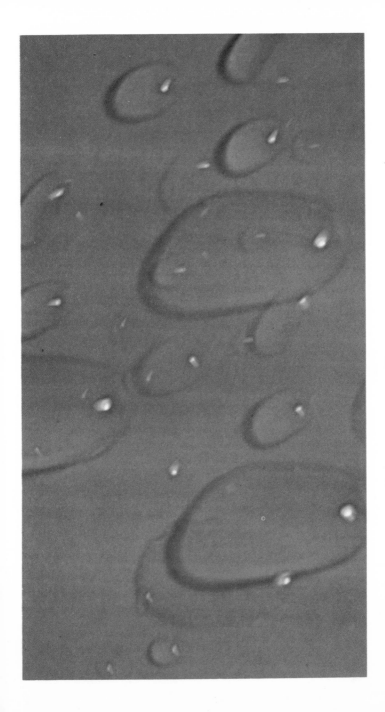

It takes two to speak the truth—one to speak, and another to hear.

Do not despair of life. Think of the fox, prowling in a winter night to satisfy his hunger. His race survives; I do not believe any of them ever committed suicide.

Things do not change; we change.

Man is the artificer of his own happiness.

Civilization created palaces, but it was not so easy to create kings.

I did not see why the schoolmaster should be taxed to support the priest, and not the priest the schoolmaster.

To be a philosopher is not merely to have subtle thoughts, but so to love wisdom as to live according to its dictates, a life of simplicity, independence, magnanimity, and trust.

For a week I heard the circling groping clangor of some solitary goose in the foggy mornings, seeking its companion. In April the pigeons were seen again flying express in small flocks, and in due time I heard the martins twittering over my clearing. . . . The tortoise and the frog are among the precursors and heralds of this season, and birds fly with song and glancing plumage, and plants spring and bloom, and winds blow.

My life is like a stroll upon the beach.

The swiftest traveller is he that goes afoot.

Shall I not rejoice also at the abundance of the weeds, whose seeds are the granary of the birds?

As I was fishing from the bank, standing on the quaking grass and willow roots, I heard a singular rattling sound. Looking up, I observed a slight and graceful hawk, alternately soaring like a ripple and tumbling a rod or two over and over, showing the underside of its wings which gleamed like a satin ribbon in the sun, or like the pearly inside of a shell. It was the most ethereal flight I had ever witnessed. It did not simply flutter or soar, but it sported with proud reliance in the fields of the air. It repeated its free and beautiful fall, turning over and over like a kite, and then recovering its lofty tumbling as if it had never set its foot on terra firma. It appeared to have no companion in the universe — sporting there alone — and to need none but the morning and the ether with which it played. It was not lonely, but made all the earth lonely beneath it.

At the same time that we are earnest to explore and learn all things, we require that all things be mysterious and unexplorable, that land and sea be infinitely wild, unsurveyed and unfathomed by us because unfathomable. We can never have enough of Nature.